What Christians
Should Know About...

Religious Spirits

Rick Joyner

Sovereign World

Scripture quotations in this publication are taken from
the New American Standard Bible,
© 1960, 1962, 1963, 1968, 1971, 1973, 1974, 1977
by the Lockman Foundation.
Used by permission.

Other Bible versions used are:
KJV – King James Version – Crown copyright
NKJV – Holy Bible, New King James Version,
© 1979, 1980, 1982 by Thomas Nelson, Inc.

ISBN: 1 85240 236 9

SOVEREIGN WORLD LIMITED
PO Box 777, Tonbridge, Kent TN11 0ZS, England.

Typeset by CRB Associates, Reepham, Norfolk.
Printed in England by Phase Print Ltd, Nottingham.

Contents

Acknowledgements

Some of the material for this article, as well as a few of the warning signs at the end, were derived from Jack Deere's outstanding audio tape series, *Exposing The Religious Spirit*, which is available through the Tape Catalogue of *MorningStar Publications*.

Acknowledgements

Part 1

Discerning the Religious Spirit

Loving God is the greatest commandment, and the greatest gift that a man can possess. The second great commandment is to love our neighbour. As the Lord affirmed, the whole Law is fulfilled by keeping these two commandments. That is, if we keep these two commandments, we will keep the whole Law. If we love the Lord we will not worship idols. If we love our neighbours we will not envy them, steal from them, or murder them, etc. Therefore, keeping these two positive commandments to love will enable us to fulfil all of the negative 'do nots' of the Law.

Simple love for God will overcome most of the evil in our hearts, and is the most powerful weapon against evil in the world. Because loving God is our highest goal, it must be the primary focus of our lives. That is why one of the enemy's most deceptive and deadly attacks upon the Church is meant to divert us from this ultimate quest. It is his strategy to keep us focused on the evil in our lives, knowing that we will become what we are beholding (2 Corinthians 3:18). As long as we keep looking at the evil, it will continue to have dominion over us. When we look to the Lord and behold His glory, we will be changed into His image.

This is not to imply that we excuse and overlook the sin and error that surfaces in our lives. In fact, the Scriptures command us to examine ourselves and test ourselves to be sure that we are still in the faith (2 Corinthians 13:5). The issue is – what do we do after the iniquity is discovered? Do we turn to the Tree of the Knowledge of Good and Evil, or to the Tree of Life? Do we try to make ourselves better so that we will then be acceptable to

God, or do we turn to the cross of Jesus to find the forgiveness, the acceptance, and the power to overcome the sin?

A primary strategy of the enemy is to keep us focused on the evil, partaking of the Tree of Knowledge, and away from the glory of the Lord and the cross. This tactic comes in the form of a religious spirit. This spirit is the counterfeit to the true love of God, and true worship. This evil spirit has probably done far more damage to the Church than the New Age Movement and all of the other cults combined.

The Nature of a Religious Spirit

A religious spirit seeks to substitute religious activity for the power of the Holy Spirit in the believer's life. Its primary objective is to have the Church *'holding to a form of godliness, although they have denied its power'* (2 Timothy 3:5). The apostle completed his exhortation with *'avoid such men as these.'* This religious spirit is the *'leaven of the Pharisees and Sadducees'* (Matthew 16:6) of which the Lord warned His disciples to beware.

When the Lord used metaphors it was because they characterised the object of the lesson. The religious spirit does operate like the leaven in bread. It does not add substance or nutritional value to the bread, it only inflates it. Such is the result of the religious spirit. It does not add to the life and power of the Church. It feeds the very pride of man which caused the first fall, and almost every fall since. Satan seems to understand even better than the Church that *'God resists the proud, but gives grace to the humble'* (James 4:6 NKJV). He knows very well that God will not inhabit any work that he can inflate through pride, and will even resist it Himself. So Satan's strategy is to make us proud, even proud of good things such as how much we read our Bibles, or witness, or feed the poor. He knows well that even if we do the will of God in pride, it will be counter-productive and will ultimately work toward our fall.

Satan also knows that once leaven gets into the bread, it is most difficult to remove. Pride, by its very nature, is the most difficult stronghold to correct or remove. A religious spirit keeps us from hearing the voice of God by having us assume that we already know God's opinion, what He is saying, and what pleases Him. This delusion is the result of believing that God is just like us. This will cause us to rationalise Scripture, having us believe that rebukes, exhortations, and words of correction are for other people, but not for us.

If this is a problem in your life, you have probably already begun to think about how badly someone you know needs to read this. It may not even have occurred to you that God put this into your hands because you need it. In fact, we all need it. This is one enemy that all of us are battling to at least some degree. It is imperative that we get free of this devastating deception and stay free. We will not he able to worship the Lord in Spirit and Truth until we do.

The degree to which we have been delivered from this powerful deception will directly affect the degree to which we will be able to preach the true Gospel in true power. The Church's confrontation with the religious spirit will be one of the epic battles of the last days. Everyone will be fighting in this battle. The only issue to be determined is on which side we will be during this battle.

We will not have the authority to deliver others from darkness if we are not free ourselves. To begin taking ground from this vast enemy, we must ask the Lord to shine His light on us, showing how this applies to us personally.

As the Lord's continuous confrontations with the Pharisees and Sadducees were an example, the Church's most desperate fight from the very beginning has been with this spirit. The primary characteristic of the Pharisees was their tendency to focus on what was wrong with others, while being blind to their own faults. The religious spirit tries to make us more prone to seeing what is wrong with others than the need for our own correction.

The Sadducees did not believe in the supernatural, which cast them into the delusion of dependency on the carnal strength and wisdom of men. This aspect of the religious spirit would have us depend on human strength and wisdom in place of the power of God. As Paul stated in 1 Corinthians 4:20, *'the kingdom of God does not consist in words, but in power.'* Our

9

God is a supernatural God who has demonstrated His supernatural power from the beginning. Whoever does not acknowledge His supernatural power as not only present, but essential for the accomplishing of His purposes today, has been deluded by a form of the religious spirit.

The spirit that operated in the Pharisees and Sadducees in the Lord's time continues to operate in religious people today. The result of both of the philosophies, which are rooted in the same Tree of the Knowledge of Good and Evil, is to replace the power of God with human wisdom, strength and righteousness. They are in direct conflict with the true work of the Holy Spirit, just as these sects so vehemently resisted the Lord Jesus Himself when He walked the earth.

The Great Deception

One of the most deceptive characteristics of the religious spirit is that it is founded upon zeal for God. We tend to think that zeal for God cannot be evil, but that depends on **why** we are zealous for Him. Paul wrote of his Jewish brethren in Romans 10:2: *'I bear them witness that they have a zeal for God, but not in accordance with knowledge.'* No one on earth prayed more, fasted more, read the Bible more, had a greater hope in the coming of the Messiah, or had more zeal for the things of God, than the Pharisees. Yet, they were the greatest opposers of God and His Messiah when He came.

The young Saul of Tarsus accurately called himself 'the Pharisee of Pharisees.' He was motivated by zeal for God while he was persecuting the Church. Zeal for God is one of the most badly needed characteristics of the Church today, which is bound by a terrible Laodicean lukewarmness. The Lord commanded the Church to *'be zealous therefore, and repent'* (Revelation 3:19). The truly zealous are the most difficult to stop, so the enemy's strategy against those that he cannot stop is to push them too far. His first step is to get them to glory in their own zeal. Regardless of how important a gift or characteristic is that we have, if the enemy can get us to take pride in it, he will have us in his snare, and we will use that gift for evil.

The Lord had little trouble with demons while He walked the earth. They quickly bowed the knee to Him, begging for mercy. It was the conservative, zealous religious community that was His greatest enemy. Those who were the most zealous for the word of God crucified the Word Himself when He became flesh to walk among them. The same is still true. All of the cults and false religions combined have not done as much damage to the true moves of God as the opposition, or infiltration, of the religious spirit. Cults and false religions are easily discerned, but the religious spirit has thwarted or diverted possibly every revival or movement to date, and it still retains a seat of honour throughout most of the visible Church.

It is a manifestation of the religious spirit that will take its seat in the very temple of God, declaring himself to be God. The temple of God is no longer made with hands, and this is not speaking about a building in Jerusalem. This man of sin will take his seat in the Church. Unfortunately, it will obviously be the Church that allows him to do this.

The 'man of sin' is a personification of the sin of man. That sin was born in man when he sought wisdom and knowledge apart from God in order to be like God. We must understand that those who are bound by a religious spirit are trying to be like God! Only they are trying to do it apart from God, His grace and His strength. The 'man of sin' is not so much an opposer of Christ as he is a substitute for Him. This is the nature of the religious spirit. It is a personification of the 'good' side of the Tree of Knowledge; it has the appearance of goodness and righteousness, but its fruit will always be death, because it usurps the true place of the cross of Christ in our lives.

The Two foundations
Like most of the enemy's strongholds, the religious spirit builds its work on two basic foundations – fear and pride. **The religious spirit seeks to have us serve the Lord in order to gain His approval, rather than from a position of having our approval through the cross of Jesus.** Therefore, the religious spirit bases relationship to God on personal discipline rather than the

propitiatory sacrifice of Christ. The motivation for doing this can be either fear or pride, or a combination of both.

Fear and pride are the two basic results of the fall, and our deliverance from them is usually a long process. That is why the Lord even gave Jezebel *'time to repent'* (Revelation 2:20–21). The biblical Jezebel was the wife of King Ahab and a very religious woman, but she was given to false religion. The Lord gave her time to repent, because the roots of this spirit go so deep that time is required to fully repent, and be delivered from it.

However, even though the Lord gave Jezebel time to repent, He rebuked the church of Thyatira for 'tolerating' her (verse 20). We can be patient with people who have religious spirits, but we must not tolerate their ministry in our midst while we are waiting! If this spirit is not confronted quickly it will do more damage to the church, our ministries, our families, and our lives, than possibly any other assault that we can suffer.

The Foundation of Guilt

Eli, the priest who raised Samuel, is a good biblical example of someone who ministers in a religious spirit founded upon guilt. Eli had so much zeal for the Lord that when he heard that the ark had been captured by the Philistines he fell over and died. He had spent his life trying to serve the Lord as the High Priest, but the very first word given to Samuel was one of the most frightening rebukes given in the Scriptures – for Eli!

> '"For I have told him that I am about to judge his house forever for the iniquity which he knew, because his sons brought a curse on themselves and he did not rebuke them. And therefore I have sworn to the house of Eli that the iniquity of Eli's house shall not he atoned for by sacrifice or offering forever."' (1 Samuel 3:13–14)

Eli's zeal for the Lord was based on sacrifices and offerings intended to compensate for his irresponsibility as a father. Guilt in our lives can stir us on to great zeal for the Lord, which usually results in the use of our sacrifices and offerings as an attempt to atone for our failures. This is an affront to the cross, which alone can atone for our guilt. Such zeal will never be acceptable to the Lord, even if we could make sacrifices forever.

We should note here that the Lord did not say that Eli's sin could not be forgiven. He just said that Eli's attempts to atone for sin by sacrifice and offering would never atone for it. There are multitudes of men and women whose zeal for the Lord is likewise based on an attempt to atone for sin, failure, or irresponsibility in other areas of their lives. But all of the sacrifices in the world will not atone for even our smallest failure. Even the attempt to try is an insult to the cross of Jesus, which alone is an acceptable sacrifice for sin.

The attempt to gain God's approval by our own sacrifice opens the door wide for a religious spirit, because our service is not based on the blood of Jesus and the power of the cross, but on an attempt to make our own atonement for sin. This does not imply that we should not do things to please the Lord, but we must keep as our motive to be pleasing the Lord for His joy, not for our acceptance. One is God-centred, and the other is self-centred, and that of the most destructive kind – an attempt to circumvent the cross.

It is also noteworthy that one of the sins of Eli's sons was that they *despised the offering of the LORD'* (1 Samuel 2:17). They appropriated the sacrifices and offerings brought to the Lord for their own selfish use. Those who are gripped by this form of a religious spirit will often be the most zealous to preach the cross, but herein is the perversion: it emphasises **their** cross more than the cross of Jesus. Their delight really is more in self-abasement than in the cross of Christ, which alone makes us righteous and acceptable to God.

The Foundation of Pride
Idealism is one of the most deceptive and destructive disguises of the religious spirit. Idealism is of human origin and is a form of humanism. It has the appearance of only seeking the highest standards and the preservation of God's glory. However, idealism is possibly the most deadly enemy of true revelation and true grace. It is deadly because it does not allow

for growing up into grace and wisdom, but attacks and destroys the foundation of those who are in pursuit of God's glory, but are not yet there.

Idealism makes us try to impose standards on others that are beyond what God has required, or of the grace that we have been given at that time. For example, men controlled by this kind of religious spirit may condemn those who are not praying two hours a day as they are. The truth is, it may be God's will for us to be praying that much, but how we get there is the difference. The grace of God will first call us to pray just ten minutes a day. Then, as we become so blessed by His presence, we will want to spend more and more time with Him until we will not want to quit after ten minutes, then an hour, then two. Then, when we are praying two hours a day, it is because of our love for prayer and the presence of the Lord, not out of fear or pride.

A religious spirit based on idealism will usually be seeking the perfect church and will refuse to be a part of anything less. Those led by the Holy Spirit may have hopes for a church that are just as high, but will still he able to give themselves in service to even some of the most lowly works in order to help those works grow in vision and maturity. The Holy Spirit is called 'the Helper', and those who are truly led by the Spirit will always be looking for ways to help, not just to stand aloof and criticise.

When a religious spirit is founded upon pride, it is evidenced by **perfectionism**. The perfectionist sees everything as black or white. This develops into extremes as it requires that every person and every teaching be either 100% right or 100% wrong. This is a standard that only Jesus could comply with, and it will lead to a serious delusion when we impose it on ourselves or others. True grace imparts a truth that sets people free, showing them the way out of their sin, or to higher levels of spiritual maturity.

A person with a religious spirit can usually point to problems with great accuracy, but seldom has solutions, except to tear down what has already been built. This is the strategy of the enemy to nullify progress that is being made, and to sow

14

discouragement that will limit future progress. This produces the mentality that, if we cannot go straight to the top of the mountain, we should not climb at all, but just 'die to self.' This is a death that God has not required, and it is a perversion of the exhortation for us to take up our crosses daily.

The perfectionist both imposes and tries to live by standards that stifle true maturity and growth. The grace of God will lead us up the mountain step by step. The Lord does not condemn us because we may trip a few times while trying to climb. He graciously picks us up with the encouragement that we can make it. We must have a vision of making it to the top, and should never condemn ourselves for not being there yet, **as long as we are still climbing**.

James said, *'we all stumble in many ways'* (James 3:2). If we had to wait until we were perfect before we could minister, no one would ever qualify for ministry. Perfect obedience and understanding should always be our goal, but such will never be found within ourselves, but only as we come to perfectly abide in the Perfect One. We do not become perfect in order to do the work of God, but we are perfected, or changed, by doing His work. When we take His yoke, which implies work, we are joined to Him and His strength. It is by this union with Him in the work that we actually find rest and refreshment for our souls.

Because we now *'see through a glass, darkly'* (1 Corinthians 13:12 KJV), or in part, we are compelled to always be open to greater accuracy in our beliefs and teachings. One of the greatest delusions of all is that we are already complete in our understanding, or 100% accurate in our perceptions or actions. Those with a religious spirit will usually both teach and claim to be open to more understanding, but usually this is done to get everyone else to be open to what they teach, while they remain steadfastly closed to others.

Jesus blessed Peter and turned the keys of the kingdom over to him just before He had to rebuke him by calling him *'Satan'* (Matthew 16:23). Right after this greatest of blessings the enemy deceived him, yet the Lord did not take the keys away from Peter. Jesus knew when He gave the keys to Peter that he was soon to even deny that he knew Him. Many years after Peter used the keys to open the door of faith for both the Jews and Gentiles, the youngest of the apostles had to rebuke him publicly because of his hypocrisy. Even so, Peter was promised that he would sit on one of the twelve thrones judging the twelve tribes of Israel. The Lord has proven that He will commission and use men long before most of us would tend to, and He knows all of the mistakes that we will make when He calls us!

It seems that the Lord's leadership style was to provide a place where His followers could make mistakes and learn from them. If we required our children to be perfectly mature while they were still children, it would actually stifle their growth and maturity by overburdening them before they could comply with our standards. That is the result of the religious spirit that is rooted in perfectionism in the Church. We must impart the vision of the high calling of God, while clearly showing the next step. We must correct mistakes, because that is how we learn, but it must be a correction that encourages and frees, not one that condemns and crushes initiative.

The Deadly Combination
One of the most powerful and deceptive forms of the religious spirit is built upon the foundation of the combination of both fear and pride. Those who are bound in this way will go through periods of deep anguish and remorse at their failures, which will result in a repentance that is simply more self-abasement, and further attempts to make sacrifices that will appease the Lord. Then they will flip to the other side, where they become so convinced that they are superior to other Christians, other groups, movements, etc., that they become unteachable and unable to receive reproof. The foundation that they stand on at any given time will be dictated more by external pressure than by true conviction.

Such a religious spirit is so slippery that it will wriggle out of almost any attempt to confront it. If you address the pride, the fears and insecurities will rise up to attract sympathy. If you confront the fear it will then change into religious pride masquerading as faith. This type of spirit will drive individuals or congregations to such extremes that they will inevitably disintegrate.

The Counterfeit Gift of Discernment

A religious spirit will usually give a counterfeit gift of discernment of spirits. The counterfeit gift thrives on seeing what is wrong with others rather than seeing what God is doing in order to help them along. Here this spirit is able to do some of its greatest damage to the Church. Its ministry will almost always leave more damage and division than healing and reconciliation. Its wisdom is rooted in the Tree of the Knowledge of Good and Evil, and though the truth may be accurate, it is ministered in a spirit that kills.

This counterfeit gift of discernment is motivated by suspicion and fear. The suspicion is rooted in such things as rejection, territorial preservation, or general insecurity. The true gift of discernment can only function with love. Any other motive than love will distort spiritual perception. Whenever someone submits a judgement or criticism about another person or group, we should disregard it unless we know that the one bringing it truly loves that person or group, and has an 'investment' of service to them.

Angels of Light

When Paul warned the Corinthians about those who ministered in a religious spirit, which sought to bring a yoke of legalism upon the young Church, he explained that:

> 'Such men are false apostles, deceitful workers, disguising themselves as apostles of Christ. And no wonder, for even Satan disguises himself as an angel of light. Therefore it is not surprising if his servants also disguise themselves as servants of righteousness.'   (2 Corinthians 11:13–15)

That Satan disguises himself as an 'angel of light' could be interpreted as a 'messenger of truth.' Satan's most deceptive and deadly disguise is to come as a servant of righteousness, using

17

truths for the purpose of destruction. He is quite skilful at quoting Scripture and using wisdom, but it is the wisdom of the Tree of Knowledge that kills. He can accurately point out what is wrong with someone else, but he always does it in such a way that tears down, not offering solutions that lead to deliverance and life.

'Angels of light', who are empowered by a religious spirit, will first look for what is wrong with someone rather than for what is right. The guise will usually be the protection of the 'sheep', truth, or the Lord's glory, but a critical spirit is an evil spirit and will always end up causing division and destruction. Criticism holds forth an appearance of wisdom, but it is pride in one of its most base forms. When we criticise someone else we are declaring ourselves to be better than they are. We may be better than others in some areas, but if we are, it is only by grace. Believers know the true grace of God will never look at how to tear others down, but how to build them up, imparting the same grace upon which they have built their lives. As an old proverb declares, 'Any jackass can kick a barn down, but it requires a skilful carpenter to build one.'

The Religious Spirit and Murder
When Adam and Eve determined to live by the Knowledge of Good and Evil they were partaking of the religious spirit. The first result of this was self-centredness – they looked at themselves. The first child born to them after partaking of this fruit was Cain, who is the first biblical model of a man controlled by the religious spirit.

Cain was 'a tiller of the ground', or earthly-minded. The religious spirit will always seek to have us focused on the earthly realm rather than the heavenly realm. This '**seed of Cain**' judges by what is seen, and cannot understand those who *'endured, as seeing Him who is unseen'* (Hebrews 11:27). In Revelation we see that the second beast comes *'up out of the earth'* (Revelation 13:11); this is because the spiritual seed of Cain are tillers of the ground. This earthly-mindedness has produced one of the most evil beasts the world will ever know.

Cain also tried to make an offering to the Lord from his own

18

labours. God rejected that sacrifice, but accepted Abel's sacrifice of the blood. The fruit of our labours will never be an acceptable offering to the Lord. This was a statement from the beginning that God would only accept the blood of the Lamb. Instead of receiving this correction and repenting, Cain became jealous of his brother, and he slew him. Those who attempt to live by their own works will often become enraged at those who take their stand on the righteousness of the Lamb.

That is why Saul of Tarsus, the 'Pharisee of Pharisees', was so enraged against Christians. They represented the greatest threat to what the Pharisees had built their whole lives on. Their very existence could not be endured. Religions that are based on works will become violent very easily. This includes 'Christian' sects, where a doctrine of works has supplanted the cross of Christ.

The Lord said that if a man just hates his brother he is guilty of murder. Those who are driven by religious spirits may try to destroy by other means than physically taking lives. Many of the onslaughts of slander instigated against churches and ministries are the ragings of this same religious spirit that caused Cain to slay his brother.

The Test of a True Messenger

In Ezekiel 37 the prophet was taken to a valley full of dry bones and asked if they could live. The Lord then commanded him to 'prophesy to the bones.' As he prophesied they came together, came to life, and then became a great army. This is a test which every true ministry must pass. The true prophet can see a great army in even the driest of bones. He will prophesy life to those bones until they come to life, and then become an army. A false prophet with a religious spirit will do little more than just tell the bones how dry they are, heaping discouragement and condemnation on them, but giving no life or power to overcome their circumstances.

Apostles and prophets are given authority to build up and tear down, but we have no right to tear down if we have not first built up. We should give no one the authority to bring correction to the people under our care unless they have a history of feeding them and building them up. Some may say that eliminates the ministry of the 'prophets', but I say that those are 'prophets' I would like to eliminate from ministry. As Jude said of them, *'These are grumblers, finding fault'* who are *'hidden reefs in your love feasts'* (Jude 11–16).

Even so, as Eli gave us an example, woe to the shepherds who feed and care for the sheep but fail to correct them. The true grace of God is found between the extremes of unrighteous fault-finding and unsanctified mercy (showing mercy toward the things that God disapproves of). Either extreme can be the result of a religious spirit.

Part 2

Masks of the Religious Spirit

The Spirit of Jezebel

Though Jezebel is a manifestation of the spirit of witchcraft, it is closely related to, and works in harmony with, the religious spirit. Many of the characteristics of these two evil spirits do overlap, and they feed off of each other. For that reason it is important to include a study of this spirit with our study of the religious spirit.

Jezebel was the ambitious and manipulative wife of King Ahab, a weak leader who allowed her to dictate policy in his kingdom. The Jezebel spirit will usually be found supplanting weak leadership. The Jezebel spirit is manipulative and usually gains its influence by seduction and by making political alliances. It will strive to be close to the centre of power, and gains its identity and satisfaction through the relationship and influence it has with those who are in power. It will usually be seemingly submissive and carry even a demeaning manner when with those who are in power, but it will usually manifest a strong control spirit and shameless presumption with others.

One of the great fallacies about this spirit is the belief that it is a spiritual problem limited to women. It is true that many women do manifest characteristics of this spirit, and there are many more female 'Jezebels', but some of the most powerful that I have ever witnessed were men. Men who use seduction or political manipulation for gaining influence and power can be just as powerful in this evil as any woman. Political 'groupies' are very often dominated by this spirit. Observe how many political staffers are fawning and servile with those who are in power, but ruthless in their relationships with each other. This same spirit can also be found in ministry staffs, and will ultimately be devastating to the ministry that tolerates this spirit.

Any woman who does not submit herself to her God-given and biblical role will take on some form of this spirit. Any man who does not take on his God-given and biblical role will either become an 'Ahab' – a weak leader who allows the Jezebel spirit to gain influence and do its destructive work, or will succumb to the aspects of this witchcraft that are manifested in the control and political spirits. The only answer and deliverance from this spirit is to return and be faithful to our God-given roles. This includes being content with our present positions without striving for influence until God gives it. One of the ways that King David established a throne that the King of Kings sits upon today was by refusing to establish his authority or position by his own hand. Those who will walk in true spiritual authority will be very careful to only take that which God gives to them.

Jezebel *'calls herself a prophetess'* (Revelation 2:20). This is often one of the telltale signs of false prophets who are operating in a religious, or Jezebel, spirit – they are preoccupied with their own recognition. Our ministry is corrupted to the degree that self-seeking and the need for recognition abides within us. One who is easily offended because he is not received by a title or claim to position should never be accepted by that title or given that position! The difference between the one who is motivated by a desire for acceptance or recognition, rather than love for the Lord and union with His purposes, is the difference between the false prophet and the true. The Lord, Himself declared:

> *'He who speaks from himself seeks his own glory* [literally, 'recognition']; *but He who is seeking the glory of the one who sent Him, He is true, and there is no unrighteousness in Him.'* (John 7:18)

Those who demand recognition for their title or position have almost certainly been self-appointed to that position. Jesus, the ultimate demonstration of true authority, was the King of Glory, but was content to be known as a carpenter from the lowest place in the land. Because He spent His life seeking to glorify the Father, the Father gave the Holy Spirit to glorify Him.

The biblical Jezebel was the greatest enemy of one of the Old Covenant's most powerful prophets, Elijah, whose ministry especially represents the preparing of the way for the Lord. The Jezebel spirit is also one of the most potent enemies of the true prophetic ministry that is given to the Church and the world in order to prepare for the return of the Lord. That is why John the Baptist was persecuted by a personification of Jezebel in the wife of Herod. The prophetic ministry is the primary vehicle through which the Lord gives timely, strategic direction to His people. Jezebel knows that removing the true prophets will make the people vulnerable to her false prophets, which always leads to idolatry and spiritual adultery. This is the enemy's ultimate strategy: to keep the bride of Christ from making herself ready for Him, thus delaying His appearing and the destruction of the evil one.

When there is a void of hearing the true voice of the Lord, the people will be much more prone to the deception of the enemy. This is why Jesus called the religious leaders of His day, 'blind guides'. These men, who knew the messianic prophecies better than anyone else in the world, could look right into the face of the One who was the fulfilment of those prophecies and think that He was sent from Beelzebub.

Jezebel's prophets of Baal were also given to sacrifice, even being willing to cut and flail themselves while seeking the manifestation of their god. A primary strategy of the religious spirit is to get the Church devoted to sacrifice in a way that perverts the command for us to take up our crosses daily. This perversion will have us putting more faith in our sacrifices than in the Lord's sacrifice. It will also use sacrifices and offerings to pressure God to manifest Himself. This is a form of the terrible delusion that we can somehow purchase the grace and presence of God with our good works.

Self-righteousness

We do not crucify ourselves for the sake of righteousness, purification, spiritual maturity, or to get the Lord to manifest Himself. Such is nothing less than conjuring. We are *'crucified with Christ'* (Galatians 2:20). If we 'crucify ourselves' it will only result in **self-righteousness**. This is pride in its most base form. It is pride in a most deceptive form, because it gives the appearance of wisdom and righteousness, of which the apostle Paul warned:

> *'Let no one keep defrauding you of your prize by delighting in self-abasement and the worship of the angels, taking his stand on visions he has seen, inflated without cause by his fleshly mind, and not holding fast to the head, from whom the entire body, being supplied and held together by the joints and ligaments, grows with a growth which is from God. If you have died with Christ to the elementary principles of the world, why, as if you were living in the world, do you submit yourself to decrees, such as, "Do not handle, do not taste, do not touch!" (which all refer to things destined to perish with the using) – in accordance with the commandments and teachings of men? These are matters which have, to be sure, the appearance of wisdom in self-made religion and self-abasement and severe treatment of the body, but are of no value against fleshly indulgence.'*
>
> (Colossians 2:18–23)

The religious spirit will make us feel very good about our spiritual condition as long as it is self-centred and self-seeking. Pride feels good; it can even be exhilarating. But it keeps all of our attention on how well we are doing, on how we stand compared to others – not on the glory of God. This results in our putting confidence in discipline and personal sacrifice rather than in the Lord and His sacrifice.

Of course discipline and the commitment to self-sacrifice are essential qualities for every believer to have, but it is the motivation behind them that determines whether we are being driven by a religious spirit or by the Holy Spirit. A religious spirit motivates through fear and guilt, or through pride and ambition. The motivation of the Holy Spirit is love for the Son of God.

Delighting in self-abasement is a sure symptom of the religious spirit. This does not mean that we do not discipline ourselves, fast, or buffet our bodies as Paul did. It is the perverted delighting in these, rather than in the Son of God, that reveals a problem.

Deceptive Revelation

Colossians 2:18–19 explains that a man with a religious spirit who delights in self-abasement will often also be given to worshipping angels and taking improper stands on visions he has seen. A religious spirit wants us to worship anything or anyone but Jesus. The same spirit that is given to worshipping angels will also be prone to excessively exalt men. We must beware of anyone who unduly exalts angels, men or women of God, or who uses visions he has received to gain influence in the church. God does not give us revelations so that people will respect us more, or to prove our ministry. The fruit of true revelation will be humility, not pride.

Of course, the Scriptures teach that Christians do have these prophetic experiences, and we are also told in Acts 2:17 that in the last days they will increase. Jesus also warned that in the last days there would be many false prophets (Matthew 24:11). Prophetic revelation is essential when the Lord gives it, and the enemy knows this very well, which is why he will raise up many false prophets. But they can be easily discerned. As Paul warned the Colossians, we should beware of those who are having such revelations and are being '**inflated**' by them.

A religious spirit will always feed our pride; whereas true spiritual maturity will always lead to increasing humility. This progression of humility is wonderfully demonstrated in the life of Paul the apostle. In his letter to the Galatians, estimated to have been written in AD 56, he declared that when he visited the original apostles in Jerusalem, they *'contributed nothing to me'* (Galatians 2:6). He was by this declaring that he had as much as they did. In his first letter to the Corinthians, written about six years later, he called himself the *'least of the apostles'* (1 Corinthians 15:9). In his letter to the Ephesians, written in about AD 61, he declared himself to be the *'the very least of all saints'* (1 Corinthians 3:8). When writing to Timothy in approximately AD 65 he declared himself to be the *'foremost of all sinners'* (see 1 Timothy 1:15), adding that he had found mercy. **A true revelation of God's mercy is one of the greatest antidotes for the religious spirit**.

We should also note that the great apostle was himself not completely free of pride in the first years of his ministry. Which one of us could claim to be free of it either? The point is, we are all growing in grace, and therefore humility. Even young apostles may exude a lot of pride, but they can still be true apostles. The key here is in which direction are we going? Are we being puffed up by our commission or accomplishments? Or are we growing in grace and humility?

The Martyr Syndrome

The martyr syndrome is one of the ultimate and most deadly delusions when combined with the religious spirit. To be a true martyr for the faith is one of the greatest honours that we can receive in this life. When this is perverted it is a most tragic form of deception. When a religious spirit is combined with the martyr syndrome it is almost impossible for that person to be delivered from his deception. At that point any rejection or correction is perceived as the price he must bear to 'stand for the truth.' This will drive him even farther from the truth and any possibility of correction.

The martyr syndrome can also be a form of the spirit of suicide. It is sometimes easier to 'die for the Lord' than it is to live for Him. Those who have a perverted understanding of the cross, glory more in death than they do in life. The point of the cross is the resurrection, not the grave.

Psychology

There is a 'self-help psychology' movement that is attempting to replace the power of the cross in the Church. Humanistically-based psychology is 'another gospel'; it is an enemy of the cross, and another form of the religious spirit. Indeed, Paul again warned us:

> *'As you therefore have received Christ Jesus the Lord, so walk in Him, having been firmly rooted and now being built up in Him and established in your faith, just as you were instructed, and overflowing with gratitude. See to it that no one takes you captive through philosophy and empty deception, according to the tradition of men, according to the elementary principles of the world, rather than according to Christ.'* (Colossians 2:6–8)

We all need 'inner healing' to some degree, but much of what is being called inner healing is nothing less than digging up 'the old man' and trying to get him healed. The answer to these deep wounds is not a procedure or a formula, but simple forgiveness. When we go to the cross and find forgiveness and true acceptance, based on the blood of Jesus, we will find a perfect love able to cast out all of our fears, and wash away all bitterness and resentment.

This seems too simple, but that is why Paul said: *'But I am afraid, lest as the serpent deceived Eve by his craftiness, your minds should be led astray from the simplicity and purity of devotion to Christ'* (2 Corinthians 11:3). Salvation is simple. Deliverance is simple. There is a major strategy of the enemy to dilute the power of the gospel by having us add to it, which is how Eve was deceived. We add to it because we just do not think that it will be acceptable unless it somehow seems brilliant or abstract. That is precisely why we must become like children to enter the kingdom.

The Lord commanded the man and woman not to eat from the Tree of the Knowledge of Good and Evil because they would die. When asked about this command, Eve replied that they could not eat from the tree *'or touch it'* (Genesis 3:3). The Lord had not said anything about not 'touching' the fruit from this tree. Adding to the commandments is just as destructive as taking away from them – anyone who thinks that he can so flippantly add to the Word of God does not respect it enough to keep it when the testing comes. If Satan can get us to add or subtract from the Word, he then knows our fall is imminent, just like it was for Eve.

There are many 'Christian' philosophies and therapies that seem wise, but are in fact attempting to be substitutes for the Holy Spirit in our lives. Some people do need counselling, and there are outstanding Christian counsellors who do lead people to the cross. Others are simply leading people into a black hole of self-centredness that will consume them, and are trying to suck in everyone else around them, too. In spite of the Christian terminology, this philosophy is an enemy of the cross of Christ.

Part 3

Summary

Basically, the religious spirit seeks to replace the Holy Spirit as the source of spiritual life. It does this by seeking to replace true repentance, which leads to grace, with a repentance based on our performance. This replaces true humility with pride.

True religion is based on loving the Lord and then loving our neighbours. True religion will have discipline and obedience, but these are founded on love for the Lord rather than the need or desire for recognition or acceptance. The wife who keeps herself in shape because she loves her husband will be easily distinguished from the one who does it because of her own ego, to draw attention to herself. The former will carry beauty with grace and dignity; the latter may be appealing, but it will be a seductive appeal that is a perversion of true love.

The religious spirit is basically a manifestation of the 'good' side of the Tree of Knowledge of Good and Evil. When Adam and Eve ate of that tree in the Garden, the first result was that they looked at themselves. Self-centredness is the poison that made that fruit deadly, and it is still the most deadly poison the serpent seeks to feed us. The Holy Spirit will always lead us into a life that is Christ-centred. The religious spirit will have us focus our attention on ourselves by seeking to base our concept of the Christian life on performance.

The Holy Spirit produces fruit by joining us to the Lord. *'For the word of the cross is to those who are perishing foolishness, but to us who are being saved it is the power of God'* (1 Corinthians 1:18). However, we must understand that this is the cross of Christ, not our own cross. We are called to deny ourselves and take up our crosses daily, but we do not glory in or try to live by the power of our own sacrifices, or by 'delighting in self-abasement.' We glory in what Jesus accomplished and the sacrifice that He made. We have our standing before God on the basis of His cross. Our ability to come boldly before the throne of God has nothing to do with whether we have had a good or a bad day, or how properly we have performed all of our religious duties. Our acceptance before God, and our ability to come into His presence, is based on one thing only – the sacrifice that Jesus made for our justification.

This does not negate the need for personal holiness, as James asserted: *'faith, if it has no works, is dead'* (James 2:17). If we are joined to Christ we will not go on living in sin. However, we do not become free from sin in order to abide in Him, **but by abiding in Him**. Jesus is the Way, the Truth, and the Life. If He is not our Life, then we do not really know the Way or the Truth either. It is the religious spirit that tries to keep Christianity in the realm of the Way and Truth while keeping us from the essential union through which Jesus becomes our Life. True Christianity does not just involve what we believe, but Who we believe.

True worship does not have as its purpose to see the Lord, but it comes from our having seen Him. When we see Him we will worship. When we see His glory we will no longer be so captivated by our own positive or negative qualities, our souls will be captured by His beauty. When the Lamb enters, even the twenty-four elders will cast their crowns at His feet (see Revelation 4:10). That is the goal of true faith – to see Him, to abide in Him, and to reveal Him.

The world is becoming increasingly repulsed by religion. However, when Jesus is lifted up all men will be drawn to Him. Because the whole creation was created through Him and for Him, we all have a Jesus-size hole in our soul. Nothing else will ever satisfy the longing of the human heart, or bring us peace, except a genuine relationship with Christ Jesus.

When we are truly joined to Jesus, living water begins to flow out of our innermost being that cannot be stopped. As more and more are freed and this water begins to flow, it will become a great river of life in the midst of the earth. Those who drink from this river will never thirst again – they will have found satisfaction for the deepest yearning of the human soul. The more we get free of this religious spirit the more pure and clear these waters will be.

Twenty-five Warning Signs of a Religious Spirit
The following is a list of some of the more obvious warning signs of the religious spirit. As stated, almost everyone is battling the religious spirit to at least some degree, and everyone's fight may be different. One may be dealing with all of the issues listed below to a small degree, and yet be more free from the yoke of the religious spirit than one who is free of most of these problems, but has serious problems with just a couple of them. Our goal must be to get completely free of any influence of the religious spirit by being completely submitted to the Holy Spirit. Apart from this complete submission to the Lord, we cannot be free from the religious spirit.

A person with a religious spirit:

1. *Will often see as his primary mission the tearing down of what he believes is wrong.* Such a person's ministry will result more in division and tearing down than in lasting works that have been built on and are bearing fruit for the kingdom.

2. *Will be unable to take a rebuke, especially from those he may judge to be less spiritual than himself.* (Think back on how you responded the last few times someone tried to correct you).

3. *Will have a philosophy that will not listen to men, but 'only to God.'* Since God usually speaks through men, this is an obvious delusion, and reveals serious spiritual pride and/or fear, both of which are roots of the religious spirit.

4. *Will be inclined to see more of what is wrong with other people, other churches, etc., than what is right with them.* John saw Babylon from the valley, but when he was carried to 'a high mountain' he saw the New Jerusalem.

If we are only seeing Babylon, it is because of our perspective. Those who are in a place of true vision will have their attention on what God is doing, not men. Criticism has the appearance of wisdom, but it is one of the most profound forms of spiritual pride. Whenever we criticise another we are by that declaring ourselves to be better than they are. We may in fact be better in some ways, but if we are it is only by grace, and pride can disqualify us from receiving God's grace (James 4:6).

5. *Will be subject to an overwhelming guilt that he can never measure up to the Lord's standards.* This is a root of the religious spirit because it causes us to base our relationship with Him on our performance rather than on the cross. Jesus has already measured up for us; He is the completed work that the Father is seeking to accomplish within us. Our whole goal in life should be simply to abide in Him.

6. *Will keep score on his spiritual life.* This includes feeling better about ourselves because we go to more meetings, read our Bibles more, do more things for the Lord, etc. These are all noble endeavours, but the true measure of spiritual maturity is getting closer to the Lord.

7. *Will believe that he has been appointed to fix everyone else.* These persons become the self-appointed watchmen, or sheriffs, in God's kingdom. They are seldom involved in building, but serve only to keep the church in a state of annoyance and agitation, if not causing serious divisions.

8. *Will have a leadership style which is bossy, overbearing and intolerant of the weakness or failure of others.* James said:

> *'But the wisdom from above is first pure, then peaceable, gentle, reasonable, full of mercy and good fruits, unwavering, without hypocrisy. And the seed whose fruit is righteousness is sown in peace by those who make peace.'*
> (James 3:17–18)

32

9. *Will have a sense that he is closer to God than other people, or that his life or ministry is more pleasing to Him.* This is a symptom of the profound delusion that we draw closer to God because of who we are rather than through Jesus.

10. *Will take pride in his spiritual maturity and discipline, especially as it compares to others.* True spiritual maturity involves growing up into Christ. When we begin to compare ourselves with others it is obvious that we have lost sight of the true goal – Jesus.

11. *Will have the belief that he or she is on the cutting edge of what God is doing.* This would also include thinking that we are involved in the most important thing that God is doing.

12. *Will have a mechanical prayer life.* When we start feeling relief when our prayer time is over, or that we have prayed through our prayer list, we should consider our condition. You will never feel relief when your conversation is over with the one you love.

13. *Will do things in order to be noticed by men.* This is a symptom of the idolatry of fearing men more than fearing God, and results in a religion that serves men instead of God.

14. *Will be overly repulsed by emotionalism.* When a person who is subject to a religious spirit encounters the true life of God, it will usually appear excessive, emotional and carnal to him. True passion for God is emotional and demonstrative, such as David exemplified when he brought the ark of God into Jerusalem.

15. *Will use emotionalism as a substitute for the work of the Holy Spirit.* This seems contradictory to the previous point, but the religious spirit will often take contradictory positions in its drive for self-preservation and exaltation.

This use of emotionalism would include such things as requiring weeping and wailing as evidence of repentance, or 'falling under the power' as evidence that one has been touched by God. Both of these can be evidence of the true work of the Holy Spirit; it is when we require these manifestations that we are beginning to move in another spirit. In the First Great Awakening, Jonathan Edwards' meetings would often have some of the toughest, most rebellious men falling on the ground and staying there for 24 hours. They got up changed, and such strange manifestations of the Holy Spirit fuelled the Great Awakenings. Even so, Edwards stated that he believed that men faking the manifestations worked more to bring an end to the Great Awakening than outright enemies of the revival!

16. *Will be encouraged when his ministry looks better than others.* We could include in this being discouraged when it seems that others are looking better, or growing faster than we are.

17. *Will glory more in what God has done in the past than in what He is doing in the present.* God has not changed; He is the same yesterday, today and forever. The veil has been removed; we can be as close to God today as anyone ever has been in the past. A religious spirit will always seek to focus our attention on works and making comparisons, rather than on simply drawing closer to the Lord.

18. *Will have the tendency to be suspicious of, or to oppose new movements, churches, etc.* This is an obvious symptom of jealousy, a primary fruit of the religious spirit, or the pride that asserts that God would not do anything new without going through us. Of course, those with such a mentality are seldom used by the Lord to birth new works.

19. *Will have the tendency to reject spiritual manifestations that he or she does not understand.* This is a symptom of pride and arrogance which presumes that our opinions are the

same as God's. True humility keeps us teachable and open, patiently waiting for fruit before making judgements. True discernment enables us to look for and hope for the best, not the worst. For this reason we are exhorted to, *'examine everything carefully; hold fast to that which is good* [not what is bad]' (1 Thessalonians 5:21).

20. *Will overreact to carnality in the Church.* The truth is that there is probably far more carnality in the Church, and a lot less of the Holy Spirit, than even the most critical person has seen. It is important that we learn to discern between the two, to be delivered from our carnality, and to grow in our submission to the Holy Spirit. But the critical person will annihilate those who may still be 60% carnal, but were 95% carnal last year and are making progress, instead of helping them along the way.

21. *Will overreact to immaturity in the Church.* There is a certain amount of immaturity that is tolerable with the Lord. My six-year-old is immature compared to my four-teen-year-old, but that is acceptable because he is six. In fact, he may be very mature for a six year old. The idealistic religious spirit only sees the immaturity without considering other important factors.

22. *Will be overly prone to base evidence of God's approval on manifestations.* This is just another form of keeping score and comparing ourselves with others. Jesus did some of His greatest miracles, such as walking on water, to be seen by only a few. He was doing His works to glorify the Father, not Himself. Those who use the evidence of miracles to testify and build their own ministries and reputations have made a serious departure from the path of life.

23. *Will be unable to join anything that he does not deem as being perfect or near perfect.* The Lord joined and even gave His life for the fallen human race. Such is the nature of those who abide in Him.

35

24. *Will be overly paranoid of the religious spirit, and quick to recognise it in others, but not himself.* We do not get free of something by fearing it, but by overcoming it with faith in Christ Jesus.

25. *Will have the tendency to glory in anything but the cross of Jesus, what He has accomplished and Who He is.* If we are building our lives, ministries, or churches on anything but these, we are building on a shaky foundation that will not stand.

Scoring on the Test

As stated, we are probably all subject to the religious spirit to at least some degree. Paul exhorted us to, *'test yourselves to see if you are in the faith'* (2 Corinthians 13:5). First, he did not tell us to 'test your neighbour,' or to 'test your pastor,' but to 'test yourselves.' Using this to measure others can be a symptom that we have a serious problem. If this chapter has given you illumination about another ministry which is causing serious problems, be sure that you use it in the Holy Spirit. Let us heed the warning to the Galatians:

> *'Brethren, even if a man is caught in any trespass, you who are spiritual, restore such a one in a spirit of gentleness; each one looking to yourself, lest you too be tempted.'*
>
> (Galatians 6:1)

Ten Things We Can Do to Get Free From the Religious Spirit

I have been somewhat reticent to try to formulate this list for obvious reasons – those who are bound by a religious spirit may tend to interpret this list in a manner that just promotes more religious activity in place of true intimacy with the Lord. However, I trust that if you have the humility to read this, the Lord will give you His grace to use this list as suggested guidelines to help us draw closer to Him.

1. **Develop a secret relationship with the Lord.** The Lord warned His disciples not to be like the Pharisees who did

36

their works to be noticed by men, but to do their works in secret before the Father. In this way we begin to put our hope and trust in our relationship with Him, not men. There is no greater security than to know that we are known by God. As the Lord warned, *'How can you believe, when you receive glory from one another, and you do not seek the glory that is from the one and only God?'* (John 5:44). Seeking glory, or recognition, from men is probably the most destructive thing we can do to true faith.

2.   **Pray that the same love with which the Father loved the Son would be in us.** The Lord Jesus Himself prayed for the same love with which the Father loved Him to be in us (John 17:26). We know that this prayer of the Son of God, who was in perfect harmony with the Father, will be answered, but we *have not* because we *ask not*. When this love replaces religious duty, our good works will greatly exceed what they would be otherwise.

3.   *'Study to show thyself approved unto God* [not men]*'* (2 Timothy 2:15 KJV). When we study the Word of God in order to demonstrate our knowledge before men, or to prove our position before men, we have departed from the Spirit of Truth that leads to truth. The Spirit of Truth came to reveal Jesus, not us. We must study His Word in order to seek Him, and to do what is approved of Him, not men. As the Lord warned the Pharisees, *'You are those who justify yourselves in the sight of men, but God knows your hearts; for that which is highly esteemed among men is detestable in the sight of God'* (Luke 16:15). If we are motivated to do the things that are highly esteemed with men, or to justify ourselves before men, we will he doing that which is detestable in God's sight.

4.   **Spend quality time alone with the Lord each day**. Endeavour, as much as it is possible, to increase this to the point where you spend more time alone with the Lord than with any other individual. When we are spending time with

Him continually we will not be so prone to the guilt that drives us to start measuring our spiritual lives by our works.

5. **Seek to hear the voice of the Lord every day**. The Lord's sheep know His voice (see John 10:27). They know His voice because they spend time with Him. If a good earthly parent seeks to spend some quality time with their children each day, how much more does the Lord seek to spend quality time with us. The quality of that time can be measured by the quality of the communication. The Lord really does want to speak to all of us each day. If we would refuse to go to bed until we have heard from Him in some meaningful way, our lives would be quickly changed. The most important thing we can do each day is to spend time with Him, and hear from Him. But do not just seek to hear the words of the Lord, but the Word Himself.

6. **Ask the Lord to give us the love for our neighbours that He has for them**. Only then will our witness and our ministry to them be pure. But we must always endeavour to love the Lord first, and most. If we love the Lord more than we do our children, or our neighbours, we will love them more than we would otherwise.

7. **Seek to turn your criticisms into intercession**. Let your first response to seeing something wrong with someone else be to pray for them, asking for grace on their behalf. If someone especially irritates you, endeavour to pray for them even more. If you make an investment in them in prayer, *'where your treasure is, there will your heart be also'* (Matthew 6:21), and you will start to genuinely love them. True spiritual authority is founded on love, so if you love them enough the Lord may be able to trust you with the ministry of truth that will set them free. Some of the greatest spiritual victories that are counted in heaven are the ones that turn enemies into friends, which turn those who dwell in darkness into children of the light. This must always be our goal.

8. **Continually ask the Lord to see His glory**. It is by seeing His glory with an unveiled face that we are changed into His image (2 Corinthians 3:17). Understanding doctrine is important, but until we see His glory it only remains doctrine. When we behold Him the doctrine will become our nature. It is not by believing in our minds, but in our hearts, that results in righteousness.

9. **Keep as one of your highest goals to manifest the sweet aroma of the knowledge of God in every place**. Like Moses, ask the Lord not to send you anywhere that His manifest presence is not going to go with you. We should only want to be where He is. And we should always behave as is befitting being in the presence of the King.

10. **When you have failed to do any of these properly, ask forgiveness** and *'forgetting those things which are behind ... press toward the mark for the prize of the high calling of God in Christ Jesus'* (Philippians 3:14 KJV).